SCIENCE ANSWERS

Light

FROM SUN TO BULBS

Heinemann Library
Chicago, Illinois

Christopher Cooper

© 2004 Heinemann Library
a division of Reed Elsevier Inc.
Chicago, Illinois

Customer Service 888-454-2279

Visit our website at
www.heinemannlibrary.com

Design: Jo Hinton-Malivoire and
        Tinstar Design Ltd
(www.tinstar.co.uk)
Illustrations: Jeff Edwards
Picture Research: Rosie Garai
    and Lizz Eddison
Originated by Dot Gradations Ltd.
Printed in China

08 07 06 05
10 9 8 7 6 5 4 3 2

**Library of Congress Cataloging-in-
Publication Data**

Cooper, Christopher (Christopher Robin),
1944-
   Light : from sun to bulbs / Christopher
Cooper.
       v. cm. -- (Science answers)
Includes bibliographical references and
index.
Contents: What is light? -- How is light
made? -- How do you see things? -- How
does light move? -- What are shadows? --
Why do things have color? -- How do
lenses help you see? -- Is there light you
cannot see?
   ISBN 1-4034-0953-6 (HC.), 1-4034-3550-2
(pbk.)
   1. Light--Juvenile literature. [1. Light.] I.
Title. II. Series.
   QC360.C63 2003
   535--dc21
                2003002505

Acknowledgments
The author and publishers are grateful to
the following for permission to reproduce
copyright material:

pp. 5, 20, 22 Photodisc; pp. 6, 11, 14
Tudor Photography; p.9 Adam Hart-Davis
/Science Photo Library;p. 10 Lawrence
Manning/Corbis; p. 12 Damien
Lovegrove/Science Photo Library; p. 13
Jeremy Horner/Corbis; pp. 15, 23 Trevor
Clifford; pp. 16, 17 Liz Eddison; p. 18
Robert Holmes/Corbis; p. 21 Willie
Maldonado/Taxi/Getty Images; p. 24 John
Durham/Science Photo Library; p. 26 Don
Herbert/Taxi/Getty Images; p. 27 Ron
Chapple/Taxi/Getty Images; p. 28
Bettman/Corbis; p. 29 Roger
Ressmeyer/Corbis.

Cover photograph of the aurora
borealis reproduced with permission
of Robert Harding.

Every effort has been made to contact
copyright holders of any material
reproduced in this book. Any omissions
will be rectified in subsequent printings if
notice is given to the publishers.

Some words are shown in
bold, **like this.** You can find
out what they mean by
looking in the glossary.

Contents

About the experiments and demonstrations

In each chapter of this book you will find a section called Science Answers. It describes an experiment or demonstration that you can try yourself. There are some simple safety rules to follow when doing an experiment:

• Ask an adult to help with any cutting using a sharp knife.

• Electric sockets are dangerous. Never, ever try to experiment with them.

Materials you will use

Most of the experiments and demonstrations in this book can be done with objects you can find in your own home. A few will need items you can buy from a hardware store.

WARNING *Never look at the sun, or at any very bright **light**, either directly or through a **telescope** or binoculars. This could permanently damage your eyesight.*

What Is Light?

The world is flooded with **light.** Even before the sun rises, its light makes the sky bright, lighting up the earth. When the sky is covered with thick clouds, the day is gloomy, but a lot of the sun's light still comes through the clouds. At night, and on dull days, you use human-made light. Electric and **fluorescent** lightbulbs light up homes and offices. Outside, street lights shine to help you find your way.

Light is all around you, but you cannot hear it or feel it. You become aware of it when it enters your **eyes.** Whenever you see an object, it is because light has traveled from that object into your eyes. Light is what makes it possible for you to see.

Where does light come from?
Some objects make the light—or most of the light—that they send out. They emit, or give out, light. Examples are the sun and stars, lightbulbs when they are turned on, fires, and fireflies. These objects are called light sources. Most objects are not light sources. They send light to your eyes after first receiving it from other objects that do give out light. This is called **reflecting** light. The moon, for example, does not give out light. You see it because it reflects light from the sun. After the sun has set, the moon still reflects light to the earth.

How far can light travel?
Light from the sun travels 93 million miles (150 million kilometers) to reach the earth. This trip takes 8 minutes and 20 seconds. But light from the farthest galaxies, or star systems, that can be seen with the naked eye has traveled for trillions upon trillions of miles and taken more than 2 million years to reach Earth. And large **telescopes** can detect very faint galaxies thousands of times farther away than these.

City lights

Modern cities blaze with light at night.
Lighting in homes and workplaces runs on
electricity that comes from power stations.

How Is Light Made?

Today most human-made **light** comes from electric lightbulbs. But humans were once dependent on candles made of animal fats and oil **lamps** burning vegetable oils. It was not until the end of the 1800s that both gas and electricity were used for lighting in the home.

How does a switch make the light come on?

Today the **incandescent** lightbulb is the major form of lighting almost everywhere. Lightbulbs contain a length of coiled wire, called a **filament,** made of a metal called tungsten. An electric current flows through this when you flip the switch. The current makes the tungsten hot, so it glows. Large bulbs that use a strong electric current are used in lighting large spaces in hotels and offices. Small bulbs that use a weak current from a battery are used in pocket flashlights.

EXPERIMENT: What makes a light bulb brighter?

HYPOTHESIS
Increasing the electric current through a lightbulb increases its brightness.

EQUIPMENT
Three 8-inch (20-centimeter) lengths of plastic-coated electric wire, two batteries, flexible metal contacts, a flashlight bulb

EXPERIMENT STEPS
1. Carefully scrape off about 1 inch (3 centimeters) of the plastic coating from each end of each piece of electric wire.
2. Twist the metal end of one piece of wire around a contact on one of the batteries.
3. Twist the end of another piece around the other contact on the battery.
4. Touch the two free ends to the contacts on the bulb. Notice how brightly the bulb shines.
5. Connect both batteries, as shown. You must attach the positive (+) terminal of one to the negative (−) terminal of the other.
6. Now touch the free ends of the wires to the bulb again.
7. Notice whether the bulb is brighter with one battery or two.
8. Write down what you saw.

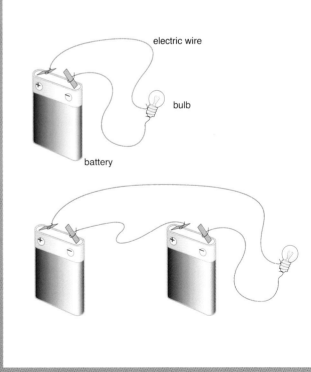

electric wire

bulb

battery

CONCLUSION
A bigger current produces a brighter light.

How Do You See Things?

You have probably seen beams of sunlight passing through curtains, window blinds, or gaps in the clouds. A very thin beam is called a ray of **light.** You can see an object when light rays are **reflected** from the object into your **eyes.**

Waves of light

Light is made up of **waves.** There are many kinds of waves around you. There are waves in water and sound waves in the air. However, light waves are different from other kinds of waves in an important way. As a water wave spreads outward, the water moves up and down at each place. This is shown by a cork, which bobs up and down as a wave passes it. But in a light wave, nothing moves. Light can travel in completely empty space, where there is no air, so there is nothing that can move.

Although nothing moves in a light wave, something is changing all the time. A light wave has electrical and magnetic effects wherever it passes. For example, a light wave can make an electric current flow when it strikes a **photoelectric cell** on a **solar-powered** calculator. This makes the calculator work. Scientists say the light wave consists of an **electromagnetic field.** The field changes in strength and direction all the time.

What happens inside your eye?

Light rays first pass through the clear front of the eyeball, or **cornea.** Behind the cornea is the **colored** part of the eye, called the **iris.** Light rays pass through the **pupil,** a hole in the iris, and then through the **lens,** a piece of **transparent** tissue. After traveling through clear liquid inside the eye, the rays finally strike the **retina,** which is at the inside back surface of the eyeball.

An eye's lens acts like the lens in a camera. It changes the direction of the light rays to form an upside-down **image,** or picture, on the retina. Thousands of nerves send **signals** from the retina to the brain. The signals carry information about the color and brightness of the light at each point in the image.

Can you see in the dark?

You cannot see when it is completely dark—that is, when there is no light at all. But the eye can improve its ability to see when there is a little light. The pupil, located in the front of the eye, can grow larger in order to let in as much light as possible.

When the light gets too bright, the pupil grows smaller to shut out some of the light. You can see the difference in a friend's pupils, or in your own, if you use a mirror. Look at the pupils indoors in faint light and then outside in sunshine.

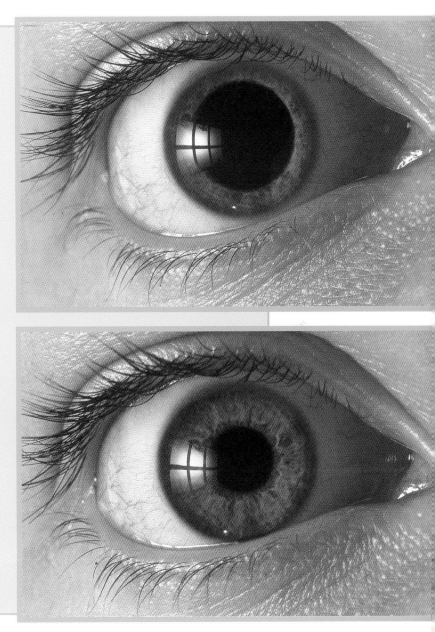

How can you tell how far away things are?

The brain has ways of figuring out how far away something is. The size of its **image** on the **retina** is important. The farther away something is, the smaller the image.

Also, the images on both retinas are slightly different. Objects appear at slightly different places in each image. When you look at a nearby object, you turn your **eyes** inward slightly so that both of them are looking directly at the object. The two images of the object are then at the same positions on the two retinas. The brain can judge the object's distance from the amount in which the eyes turn in.

Defending against glare

You can often be overwhelmed by sunlight that is too bright. Sunglasses block some of the light from passing through to your eyes. Because less light reaches the eyes, the scene looks less bright, although it is bright enough for most activities.

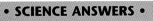

EXPERIMENT: How does the eye bend light rays?

HYPOTHESIS
Rounded, **transparent** objects (such as eyeballs and eye **lenses**) change **light** rays and form images.

EQUIPMENT
A drinking glass with straight sides, filled with water

EXPERIMENT STEPS
1. Pour water into the glass. Hold objects up behind the glass. Use pictures, printed words, patterns, your own hand.
2. Write down how the water and glass affect the appearance of the objects.
3. Change the distance between the glass and the objects behind it. Write down the result.
4. Repeat this with glasses of other sizes, if you have any.

CONCLUSION
You should have noticed that the water in the glass changed the appearance of objects behind the glass. It made things that were close look larger than they really are. Objects farther away looked as if they had been flipped from left to right. At the edges of the glass, the objects' shapes looked so different that the objects were hard to recognize. Those changes were the result of light rays bending as they passed through the water-filled glass.

The eyeball is also curved, although it is shaped like a globe, not a cylinder as the glass is. The lens of the eye has a curved shape, too. The lens and the front part of the eye bend light rays that enter the eye. Unlike the glass, they have just the right shape and size to form an image on the retina.

11

How Does Light Move?

When a **light** ray reaches a mirror, the **reflected** ray bounces off the mirror in the same line of direction that the first ray made when it reached the mirror. Just as the original light rays spread out from the object, the reflected rays spread out as if coming from a place behind the mirror. However, because the rays have been reflected, they appear to be opposite in the mirror. This is called a mirror **image.**

When you cross a street, you rely on cars to travel in the direction they seem to be going. You believe they are going in the direction from which the light has come, because light travels in straight lines. And that is true most of the time. But sometimes the direction of light rays changes, and things seem to be in the wrong places. This is the "trick" mirrors can play.

Most objects have rough surfaces that reflect light **waves** in all directions. Mirrors have very smooth surfaces, which reflect the light in a special way. It looks as if there is an object behind the mirror. You might call this a reflection of the object, but the proper name is image.

A mirror made of air

In the desert, a layer of hot air near the ground can act like a mirror. It reflects the sky, just as the surface of a lake would. This has often confused travelers. The image is called a **mirage.**

What is funny in the Hall of Mirrors?

A distorting mirror at a carnival has a wavy surface. The top part of the mirror may form an image of your head that is wider than normal, while the part just below may form an image of your chest that seems even wider. So in the mirror, your head and neck seem to be stretched out. This is because the light that hits the mirror at different places is reflected from the surface in different directions.

How fast does light travel?

When you switch on a **light,** it only takes a hundred-millionth of a second for light to flood the room. This is because light travels at a fantastic **speed,** almost 186,282 miles (299,792 kilometers) per second.

Can light bend?

Light travels more slowly in **transparent** materials, such as glass, water, or air, than it does in a vacuum (space without any air in it). In water, its speed is 3/4 of its speed in a vacuum. In glass, it is about 2/3 of that speed. In air, the speed of light is only a tiny bit slower than its speed in a vacuum.

Light rays bend whenever they change speed. For example, light bends and slows down when it passes from air into water. This bending causes a straw or a spoon to look bent when it is dipped in a transparent liquid such as a glass of water.

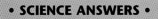
EXPERIMENT: What effects do differently shaped mirrors have on images?

HYPOTHESIS
Differently curved surfaces will distort **images** in different ways.

EQUIPMENT:
A large, shiny spoon (a soup ladle is even better), an ordinary flat mirror

EXPERIMENT STEPS
1. Hold the spoon or ladle in front of you. Look into the outside of the bowl of the spoon or ladle. This is the **convex** side. Move the ladle or spoon closer to your **eye** and then farther away. Notice what happens to the image.
2. Now look into the inside of the bowl of the spoon or ladle, the **concave** side. Move the ladle or spoon closer to your eye and then farther away.
3. Now hold the spoon in front of the flat mirror.
4. Write down what you saw.

CONCLUSION
A convex mirror gives an image that is the right way up but smaller than one made by a flat mirror.
A concave mirror produces a **magnified** image of you when you are very close. When you are far away, the image is upside-down and smaller than the one made by an ordinary mirror.

15

What Are Shadows?

A **shadow** is not a real object. It is just a place—on the ground or a wall or some other surface—that is receiving less **light** than the area around it. It is receiving less light because something is blocking off some of the light rays. Light cannot get into the shadow area because to do so it would have to bend around the object. Light generally travels in straight lines.

For example, when you stand outdoors in the sunlight, light cannot pass through your body. Some is **reflected** and some is **absorbed** by your body. There is an area on the ground that this light does not reach. This is your shadow.

Why are shadows not completely dark?

You can still see things on the ground where your shadow is. This is because some light is able to get to that place. The light comes from the sky or is reflected from surrounding buildings and other objects.

Does everything block light?

All materials block some light, but the amount varies. Some materials let through a lot of light but make things look fuzzy and blurred. Such materials are called **translucent.** An example is "frosted" glass, which has a rough surface and is often used for bathroom windows. Other examples are flimsy fabrics such as muslin.

A material that completely blocks light is called **opaque.** An object or material that lets through most of the light, such as a window, is called **transparent.** Air and clear water are also transparent. But even the most transparent materials absorb and reflect a little of the light. If a ray of light passes through several pieces of glass, each piece of glass absorbs a little more of the light. Things seen through several pieces of glass look darker than things seen through one piece.

Why are shadows different lengths?

Shadows have different lengths depending on where the **light** source is that is creating the shadow. You can see the effect by holding a desk **lamp** in the air and moving it above different objects. Some shadows will be shorter than the objects. Others will be longer, depending on where the lamp is shining. The sun has the same effect. When the sun is high in the sky, shadows are short. When the sun is lower in the sky, shadows are long.

Telling time from the sun

Sundials were once widely used to tell time. This modern sundial is a fun feature in a park.

DEMONSTRATION: MAKE A SUN DIAL AND USE IT TO TELL TIME.

EQUIPMENT
A stick at least 24 inches (60 centimeters) long; ten white stones or other markers; a watch, clock, or portable radio to get the exact time; a waterproof marker

DEMONSTRATION STEPS
1. Set the stick upright in the soil in an unused part of your yard or nearby park.
2. Draw part of a circle about 3 feet (1 meter) from the stick on its northern side (on the southern side if you live south of the equator). An adult can help with this.
3. On each hour of a sunny day, mark the point on the circle that the stick's shadow is pointing toward (if the shadow is short) or where the shadow crosses it (if the shadow is long).
4. Press a marker into the ground at this point and label it with the hour (10 A.M., 11 A.M., etc.).
5. On each sunny day after that, compare the time shown by the sundial with the correct time.
6. Draw a table showing how much the sun is ahead of or behind the true time through the year.

EXPLANATION
This simple sundial is accurate at some times of the year, but more than an hour wrong at others. The sun itself can be up to about 15 minutes ahead or behind the true time at different times of year! (This is because of the varying **speed** of the earth in its orbit around the sun.)

Why Do Things Have Color?

The **colors** you see depend on the **light** that enters your **eyes.** If the light entering your eyes from the cover of a book lying on the table is red (or mostly red) and if your eyes are working normally, then the book looks red.

Sunlight is a mixture of light **waves** of many different colors. This mixture looks white to the human eye. If an object **reflects** all of these colors when the reflected light enters a human eye, the object looks white. But the red book **absorbs** some of the colors of light and reflects the red light. That is why it looks red.

If another book next to the red book reflects mainly green light and absorbs other colors, then it looks green.

Bright and beautiful

National flags use bright, rich colors so that they stand out and attract the attention of onlookers. You could not see any of these colors if they were not already present in the sunlight that falls on the flags.

Why do things look different in colored light?

You can change the color that an object appears by changing the color of the light that shines on it. If you put a red bulb into a **lamp,** the appearance of the objects in the room will change. The green book will not be able to reflect any green light, because there is almost no green light reaching the book from the red bulb. So the green book will reflect very little light and will look black. But the red book will reflect the red light from the bulb and will look much as it looks in ordinary light. The white paper will also reflect the red light and will look red. If a green bulb is used, the green book and the paper will both look green, and the red book will look black.

Can colors be separated?

Sunlight is white **light.** The **colors** mixed up in sunlight often become separated. Light is **refracted** as it enters glass, water, or a gemstone. Violet rays are refracted the most, red rays the least, and other colors by in-between amounts. If the material is angled like the faces of a gemstone (such as a diamond), or curved like a water droplet, the colors are separated even more after the light passes through the material.

When this separated light shines on a wall or other surface, it forms a band of multicolored light called a **spectrum.** A **rainbow** is a spectrum, too. Rainbows are formed when sunlight is refracted and separated into different colors when it passes through raindrops.

EXPERIMENT: How can you find out what colors of light are reflected by an object?

HYPOTHESIS
Transparent colored materials show each color in the **reflected** light separately.

EQUIPMENT
Some different colored filters (these are materials that let through only some colors, such as transparent colored candy wrappings, colored gift wrap, or pieces of colored plastic)

EXPERIMENT STEPS
1. Place a few colorful objects in a bright light. The objects can be things such as different-colored candy or buttons.
2. View each object through each of your filters.
3. Make a table with columns titled "Object," "Filter Color," and "Brightness."
4. In the "Brightness" column, write "bright," "medium," or "dark" to show how bright each object looks through each filter.

CONCLUSION
Suppose you find that a blue object looks bright through a blue filter. That means that the object reflects mainly blue light. If it looks dark through a red filter, then it reflects only a little red light. You might find that it looks medium bright through a green filter. This explains why the object looks blue. Blue light is the main part of the **spectrum** of colors in the light that it sends to your **eyes.**

23

How Do Lenses Help You See?

Cameras, **microscopes, telescopes,** eyeglasses, and even the human **eye** all use **lenses** to make **images.** Lenses are pieces of **transparent** material shaped to bend **light** rays in special ways. A **magnifying** glass is a single lens. Eyeglasses consist of two lenses held in a frame.

How do lenses work?

If you have eyeglasses, or if you can borrow a pair, you can see how they affect the way things look. You can do this by just holding the eyeglasses up to your eyes. Some lenses act as magnifying glasses do and make things look bigger. Others have different shapes and make things look smaller.

How can you see things that are very small?

Microscopes allow you to see objects that are far too small for human eyes to see. Microscopes consist of many lenses, very accurately shaped and positioned. They bend the light rays that come from a small object underneath the microscope. To the person looking through a microscope, the light rays seem to be coming from a large object. This picture shows tiny plant cells as seen through a microscope.

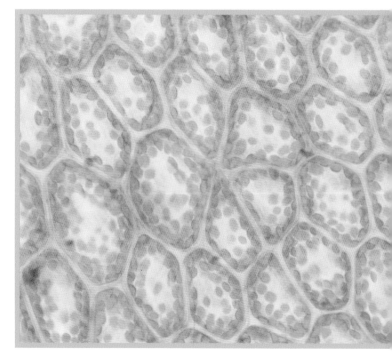

EXPERIMENT: How can you make a magnifying glass stronger?

HYPOTHESIS
Two magnifying glasses are stronger than one.

EQUIPMENT
Two inexpensive magnifying glasses from a toy store

EXPERIMENT STEPS
1. Look at some nearby objects with one of the magnifying glasses. Notice how much the objects seem bigger in size.
2. Notice the effect of holding the lens far from an object. It makes an upside-down image that appears to be between you and the lens.
3. Examine this image using the second magnifying glass. Depending on where you hold the second lens, you can form a final image that is either right-side up or upside-down and bigger than the first image.
4. Now hold the two lenses together as if they were one lens and see how much they magnify.
5. Write down what you saw.

CONCLUSION
Two lenses can be more powerful than either one by itself, depending on how they are positioned in relation to each other.

Is There Light You Cannot See?

About 2,000 years ago, scientists were amazed when they discovered **invisible light.** In fact, most of the light that comes from the sun and from lamps is invisible.

What is beyond the spectrum you can see?

When your skin gets tanned, the color is caused by an invisible part of the sunlight. This light is called **ultraviolet (UV) light.** *Ultraviolet* means "beyond violet." UV light is called this because when sunlight is spread out into a **spectrum,** the invisible ultraviolet rays occur just outside the spectrum, next to the violet rays that you can see. The ultraviolet light can be detected because it causes changes on photographic film as well as skin.

You cannot see ultraviolet light, but many other creatures, such as birds and bees, can.

Dangers of UV

When UV light from sunlight reaches your skin, it passes into the skin. Cells in the skin make a dark substance called melanin, which blocks the UV light and protects the body. Exposure to too much UV light is dangerous and can cause skin disease later in life. The risk is reduced if people avoid the sun, by staying in the shade and keeping the skin covered in the middle of the day, when sunlight is brightest. Sunblocks and sunscreens help a little by blocking out some of the UV light.

Heat radiation

Beyond the red light at the other end of the spectrum is invisible infrared (IR) light—usually called **infrared radiation**. (*Infrared* means "below red.") You can feel IR radiation as warmth on your skin. Infrared rays come from all the objects around you, including your own body. The warmer an object is, the more IR radiation it sends out. It is possible to take photographs and make television pictures using the infrared radiation from a scene. Remote control units control TV sets and other electronic equipment with pulses of infrared radiation.

People Who Found the Answers

Thomas Young (1773–1829)

The English doctor and scientist Thomas Young was a brilliant student at school. He knew many languages. When he was studying to become a doctor and was learning about how the **eye** works, he became interested in light. He showed that muscles in the eye change the shape of the **lens** in order to focus on objects.

Young suggested that the eye has three kinds of light-sensitive detectors, each triggered most strongly by particular **colors** of light. The different strengths of the **signals** that they send to the brain produce all the different color sensations. Young also did experiments in which he showed that light consists of **waves.**

Jean-Bernard-Léon Foucault (1819–1868)

Foucault studied the **speed** of light, bouncing a beam of light off a spinning mirror. He saw that light would travel to a fixed mirror a few feet away and be reflected back the way it came. But when the mirror was spinning very fast, it moved through a tiny "space" between the moment when the light was **reflected** from the revolving mirror and the moment it returned to the fixed mirror. The light was reflected at an angle in this space. He measured this angle to figure out the speed of light. He arrived at the value of 185,168 miles (298,000 kilometers) per second—very close to the correct figure of 186,282 miles per second.

Amazing Facts

- Light waves have an extremely short **wavelength.** Red light has the longest wavelength, but even this is only a tiny fraction of an inch. Violet light has the shortest wavelength, which is about half of the wavelength of red light.

- The distance to the moon has been measured by bouncing light from it. The astronauts who visited the moon between 1969 and 1972 left mirrors there, pointing toward the earth. Later, flashes of light from powerful **lasers** were fired from the earth. The reflected light took about 2.5 seconds to travel the approximately 239,000 miles (384,000 kilometers) to the moon and then back again. Scientists measured the time very accurately and so found the distance to within a few inches.

- Some animals can feel **infrared radiation** far more accurately than humans can. Some types of snakes, including pit vipers, rattlesnakes, and pythons, have infrared-detecting organs in their heads. The snakes can detect the warmth from their prey, such as mice, when it is too dark to see anything by visible light.

- You can sometimes see the **shadow** of the earth. At times, the moon enters Earth's shadow. It is then partly or completely darkened, because the moon shines only by reflecting the light of the sun. This is called an eclipse of the moon. In some years there are no eclipses of the moon. In other years there can be one, two, or even three.

# Glossary

absorb   take in, swallow up. Most objects absorb some light, while the rest of the light bounces back or passes through.

color   sensation produced by the eye and brain when light enters the eye. Color depends on the various wavelengths in the light.

concave   curved like the inside of a bowl, with the center farther away from the viewer than the outside

convex   curved like the outside of a bowl, with the center closer to the viewer than the outside

cornea   clear front part of the eyeball

electromagnetic field   pattern of electrical and magnetic influences. An electromagnetic field can make electric currents flow or affect magnets. Light waves consist of fast-changing electromagnetic fields.

eye   organ in humans and many other animals that detects light

filament   in an electric lightbulb, a hot glowing metal wire

fluorescent   describes a lightbulb that consists of a hollow tube filled with gas at low pressure. When an electric current passes through the gas, the gas gives out invisible ultraviolet (UV) light. A special material that coats the inside of the tube absorbs the ultraviolet light and gives out visible light.

image   picture of something

incandescent   hot and glowing

infrared radiation   waves that are like visible light, but they have wavelengths too long to be seen by the human eye

invisible   not able to be seen

iris   colored part of the eye that controls how much light is let in

lamp   device that contains something that produces light, such as burning oil or gas or a glowing metal wire

laser   device that produces a beam of light that is of one very precise wavelength

lens   piece of **transparent** material shaped to bend the path of light rays so that they form an image

light   waves to which the eyes are sensitive, allowing people to see the surrounding world; also applied to ultraviolet and infrared waves

magnify   make something look bigger

microscope   instrument that has lenses arranged to make small objects appear larger

mirage misleading appearance of something in the distance caused when light rays are bent as they travel through layers of air of different temperatures

opaque not letting light through

photoelectric cell device that generates electricity when light strikes it

pupil hole in the iris at the front of the eye through which light enters the eye

rainbow curved band of glowing colors formed in the sky when sunlight is reflected and refracted by raindrops

reflection light that is bounced back when it strikes a surface

refraction bending of light when it travels from one material into another

retina layer at the back of the eye that is sensitive to light

shadow place that receives less light than nearby places because some light is blocked out by an opaque object

signal in nerves, signals are electric currents that carry information to the brain about what is happening in the body

solar powered describes something that gets its energy from sunlight

spectrum band of color produced when a beam of light is spread out so that the different wavelengths in it are separated; range of different wavelengths produced when any waves—light, infrared, ultraviolet, or others—are spread out according to their wavelengths

speed how fast something moves. Light speed is measured in miles (or kilometers) per second.

telescope instrument that contains lenses or mirrors arranged to make distant objects look closer

translucent describes a material that you can see through, but not clearly, like muslin or "frosted" glass

transparent describes a material that you can see through clearly, like ordinary window glass

ultraviolet (UV) light waves that are like visible light, but with wavelengths too short to be seen by the human eye

wave a disturbance of an electromagnetic field

wavelength distance from one crest of a wave to the next

Index

More Books to Read

Hewitt, Sally. *Fascinating Science Projects: Light.* Brookfield, Conn.: Millbrook Press, Inc., 2002.

Gareth Stevens Publishing Staff. *Light.* Milwaukee, Wis.: Gareth Stevens Inc., 2003.

Parker, Steve. *Science Fact Files: Light and Sound.* Austin, Tex.: Raintree, 2000.